Flying in Faith with Etty and Esty

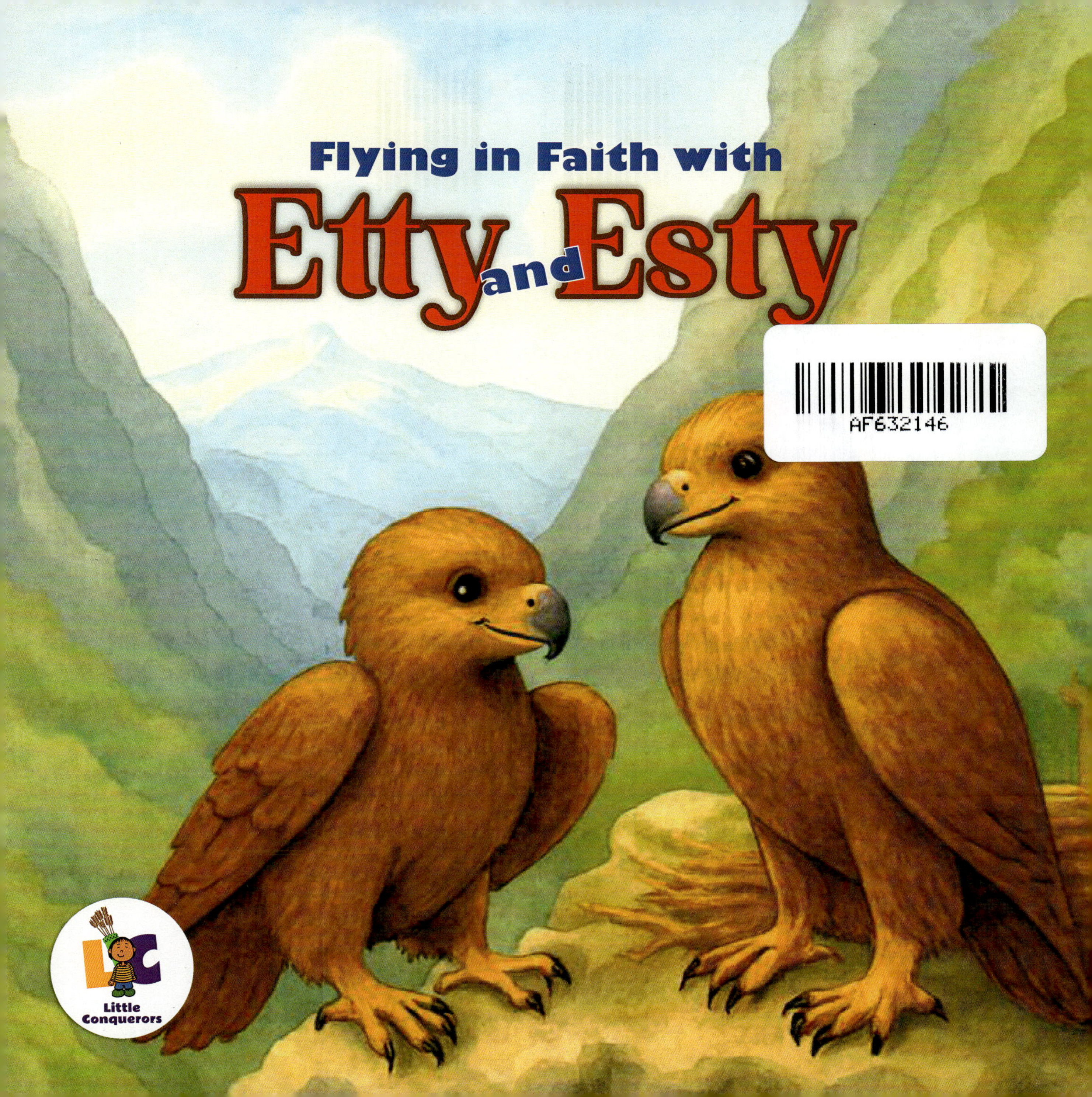

Little Conquerors

OrangeBooks Publication

1st Floor, Rajhans Arcade, Mall Road, Kohka, Bhilai, Chhattisgarh 490020

Website:**www.orangebooks.in**

First Edition, 2025

ISBN: 978-93-7426-825-4

Price: Rs. 350.00

Printed in India

This book belongs to

CHAPTER 1

Wings of Love

High up on the mountain cleft, where the winds whistled and the clouds cuddled, lived two fearless golden eagles – Ethan and Ella. They were huge birds with strong wings and sharp talons.

Whoosh! They soared high through the sky. With a swoop and a dive, they wheeled high and free, exploring the landscape below.

DYK

Golden Eagles have a super cool science name: ***Aquila Chrysaetos.* They have fierce feet!** Their **talons** are sharp, curved claws that help them catch animals to eat.

In their cozy nest, nestled among the rocky peaks, were their two little eaglets, Esty and Etty.

Ethan and Ella cared for them with all their heart. They brought them food, kept them warm, and protected them from danger.

DYK

Golden Eagles build **big, strong nests** high up on cliffs or tall trees. They use **sticks, grass, and moss** to make their cozy homes.

One winter night, the swift winds howled through the mountains. Ella ruffled the twigs closer together in the nest tucking them in close for warmth. Ethan glided through the sky.

SWOOP! He darted down towards the nest.

What did he see?

DYK

Their wings are **HUGE!** When they stretch them out, they can be as wide as a grown-up bed—up to **7.4 feet (2.3 meters)!**

Ethan landed near the nest, his golden feathers shining in the fading light. "Ella, I sense a storm coming," said Ethan.

"Yes, Ethan, I sense that too," said Ella, "Don't worry I got the little ones safe."

She gently pulled Esty and Etty closer to her and wrapped her wings around them. Ethan took shelter behind a rock but his eyes were on the nest. He was watching—ready to protect his family.

The cold winds grew fiercer, shaking the trees and rattling the loose rocks. But Ella did not move. She sat in the nest wrapping her wings around her little ones.

DYK

The mama eagle lays **1 to 3 eggs** each year, and they hatch after **about six weeks**.

The storm got worse. Whoosh! Whoosh! The icy cold winds whipped through the mountains and Ella couldn't hold longer.

"I'm tired, Ethan," Ella called. "I can't sit much longer."

Ethan flapped his mighty wings and soared to the nest. "I'm here now—I'll take care of them. You rest."

Ella nodded and stepped aside. Ethan, holding his little ones closer to him, he sat in the nest and wrapped them around his huge, strong wings.

The wind howled all through the night, but inside the nest, the eaglets were warm and safe under Ethan's wings.

DYK

During big storms—especially with **hail**—Golden Eagles find safe places to hide.

At dawn the storm calmed down and the sky turned bright. The golden sun peeked over the mountains, sending its first warm rays onto the rocky cliffs.

"Kee-yep, Kee-yep," the eaglets chirped softly.

Ethan smiled, "It is alright my little ones; do not be afraid the storm has gone. You are safe under my wings."

The eaglets snuggled close, feeling warm and protected. The winds had passed, and a new day had begun.

"...like an eagle that stirs up its nest and hovers over its young, that spreads its wings to catch them and carries them aloft," the Lord will lead you – Deuteronomy 32:11

DYK

Golden Eagles usually live alone or in pairs, and their home area can be **as big as 200 square kilometers**—that's like hundreds of football fields!

Chapter 2

Wait for the Best

Months passed by, Etty and Esty had grown fluffier and stronger. They didn't need to be fed anymore; they could eat the food their parents brought them.

"Kee-yep! Kee-yep!" cried Etty and Esty, "We are hungry."

"Yes, Yes, my little ones, we will bring you some food," said Ella

"You stay home, Ella. I will get some food," said Ethan

"Alright, come back soon," said Ella

DYK

Young eagles stay in their nest for **three months.** After they learn to fly, their parents still feed them for a long time—up to **six months!**

Ethan spread his huge wings – FLAP! FLAP! Up, up he went soaring higher and higher into the sky.

"Kee-yep! Look how high Dad is flying," squealed Etty wide-eyed in wonder.

"Yea! So high! But Mom, how will Dad find food from so high?" asked Esty.

"My dear, we eagles are gifted with super sharp eyesight! When we're flying way up high, we get a good view of all the sides and we can spot everything clearly. That helps us find food!" said Ella

DYK

Golden eagles have super sharp eyes! They can see about 8 times better than humans! From way up high in the sky, they can spot tiny movements and even see animals more than a mile away.

"Wow! I can see Dad!" Esty squealed, bouncing with excitement.

"And look—there's a hare down below!" shouted Etty, "Come on Dad, catch it."

"See? From here on the cliff, you can see clearly far down below," said Ella

"But why isn't Dad diving down?" Esty asked, her feathers twitching.

"Be patient Esty," Ella said with a knowing smile.

DYK

Golden eagles hunt animals like rabbits, birds, and sometimes even bigger ones like foxes and deer. **They're strong and fast!**

"Oh no! Esty shouted, "The hare is running into the burrow. Hurry Dad! Catch it!"

But Dad was soaring peacefully, and the hare disappeared.

"Gone!" said Esty sadly.

"Ahh!" sighed Etty.

Ella watched her eaglets, smiling at their excitement and disappointment.

DYK

Golden eagles soar way up in the sky. They're very patient and when the **time is just right**, they zoom down fast to grab their food—like a surprise swoop!

"I am hungry Mom!" Esty grumbled.

"Me too!" said Etty in a soft voice.

"Dad is still flying around, and he is not catching anything!" Esty huffed.

"Wait, my dear," said Ella calmly, "Dad is waiting for the right time."

"But when? I want food now!" said Esty impatiently.

"Kee-yep! Kee-yep!" "Kee-yep! Kee-yep!", both the eaglets screeched, flapping their wings.

Etty and Esty flapped their wings and chirped in frustration. "Why is Dad just circling up there?" they screeched.

Suddenly—WHOOSH!

Like a flash of lightning, Ethan dived down swiftly. But wait! – instead of heading towards the burrows. He was flying towards the river bushes.

The eaglets blinked in surprise, their beaks wide open. What was he doing?

Then—SNATCH!

His talons struck, lifting a fluffy hare from the grass. Up, up, up he soared, the wind rushing past his feathers.

FLAP! FLAP! FLAP!

Higher and higher he climbed, circling the sky like a proud hero. And with one final swoop, Ethan glided back home, the hare still tight in his grip.

DYK

Golden eagles are super-fast, faster than a roller coaster! They can zoom through the air at 150 miles per hour, making them one of the **fastest animals on Earth!**

Etty and Esty stared wide-eyed as Dad landed on the cliff, looking majestic.

"Food!" they squealed and rushed to eat.

Once their bellies were full, Esty asked, "Dad, why did you take so long to catch the hare? We were watching you the whole time!"

Ethan smiled. "There were many hares around and I was looking out for the right one. If I had dived too quickly, all the hares would get alert and run," he explained. "I had to stay focused, be patient, and strike at the perfect moment. I had to wait for the right time to get the best for you."

"The Lord satisfies your desires with good things so that your youth is renewed like the eagle's." - Psalm 103:5

Chapter 3

Born to Soar

Whoosh! Whoosh! Etty and Esty swooped down and landed roughly on the cliff. They had been practising their flying for days, and now they were getting really good at it!

"Bravo, my little ones!" cheered Mama Ella, her eyes sparkling with pride. "You're flying so well!"

"Thank you, Mom!" chirped Esty, flapping happily. "It feels amazing to soar so high!"

Mama Ella turned to Etty with a curious smile. "Etty, my dear," she said, "I've noticed you sometimes fly off on your own and then pop back suddenly. Where do you go?"

DYK

Young eagles don't fly right away. They stay near their nest for weeks or even months, practicing how to fly, hunt, and find food—all with help from their parents! This is called **fledgling.**

"Um... Mom, I made a new friend," Etty said softly.

"A new friend?" Ella asked, tilting her head. "Who is it?"

"Ray, the raven," Etty replied. "He lives in the trees below. He's really nice, and he knows lots of things. I like listening to him."

Mama Ella's feathers ruffled gently in the breeze. "Etty, my dear," she said kindly, "It's wonderful to meet new friends and learn new things. But remember—some things others say aren't always true. Especially if they're talking about you. So be wise, and choose your friends with care."

Etty nodded slowly. "Okay, Mom... I'll be careful," he whispered.

But inside, Etty felt a little sad. He didn't like what Mama had said.

DYK

Eagles have big, heavy wings. Instead of flapping a lot, they learn to soar—gliding smoothly through the sky. They wait for strong winds called **thermals** to lift them up, like riding a giant invisible elevator!

Days went by, and after each flying lesson, Etty would flutter down to the trees to visit his new friend, Ray the raven.

"I want to fly higher—just like my dad," Etty said one afternoon.

Ray's eyes widened. "Oh no, Etty! That's much too risky," he warned. "The air gets thin way up there. It's not safe!"

"Really? But I thought—" Etty began, but Ray quickly interrupted.

"Hey Etty, can I come watch you practice flying tomorrow?" he asked eagerly.

"Of course!" chirped Etty with a happy flap. "Meet me in the morning—I'll be waiting!"

With a swoosh and a smile, Etty soared back up to the cliff.

DYK

Eagles fly way up high, much higher than smaller birds like ravens. **They like flying solo** and don't hang out with little birds.

Early the next morning, Etty and Esty flapped their wings, ready for another flying lesson. They were excited to learn something new!

Ethan glided down beside them, smiling proudly. "My brave little ones," he said, "We're born to fly high. The higher we soar, the safer we are. You're doing great—but today, let's go even higher!"

Etty looked unsure. "But Dad... doesn't the air get thinner up there?"

Ethan nodded. "Yes, it does. But we're built to breathe just fine, even way up high!"

"Wow!" said Esty. "I want to try!"

"Stay close and follow me," said Ethan, lifting off into the sky. Esty zipped after him.

Etty paused, remembering Ray's warning. "Come on, Etty!" Esty called.

Just then, Ray swooped in beside them. "This is amazing!" he said.

"Glad you came!" Etty smiled, and together they flew into the morning sky.

DY

Sometimes, eagles sit and wait for days until the perfect wind comes. When it does, they jump into the sky and ride the wind like a roller coaster, mixing gliding and flying to get where they want to go.

They were having a wonderful time flying together when suddenly the sky turned dark. Cold winds blew, and thunder rumbled through the clouds.

"A storm is coming!" called Ethan. "Ray, head home! Etty, Esty—stay close and fly higher!"

Ray's eyes widened with fear. "No, Etty! It's too dangerous up there," he cried, flying close. "Come down with me—I'm scared to go alone."

Ray clung to Etty's back. "Let's go!" he urged.

"Ouch! Ray, you're hurting me," Etty said. "Please get off!"

"Don't go, Etty!" Esty called from above. "Dad said to fly higher!"

"Don't go higher!" Ray repeated. "It's not safe!"

Etty hovered in the wind, torn between Ray's fear and his father's voice. He didn't know who to trust.

DYK

Eagles can sense when a storm is coming! Instead of hiding, they fly to high places and catch the rising winds. These winds help them soar above the storm, saving energy while the storm rumbles below.

SCREECH! A loud cry from above snapped Etty out of his thoughts. He looked up.

“DAD!” he shouted back.

The storm was growing wild—rain poured, lightning flashed, thunder roared.

“Quick, Etty!” shouted Ethan. “Fly higher! You can do it! Look at me—soar above the storm!”

Etty turned to Ray. “Get off my back! I'm going to my Dad,” he said firmly.

“No! I won't!” Ray cried, holding on tight.

DYK

Ravens sometimes bother eagles—landing on their backs and pecking at them! But eagles don't fight back.

Just then, Mama Ella flew close to Etty. "Don't listen to Ray," she said gently. "Fly high, my dear. Don't stop, don't look back. Use all your strength and soar!"

Etty took a deep breath. He focused, flapped hard, and soared upward. Through the roaring clouds and stinging rain, he flew—fearless. He could see his dad ahead, shining like a beacon.

"STOP! Etty, don't go higher!" Ray shouted. "It's not safe!"

"Get off, Ray," Etty said firmly. "My Dad knows what's best for me."

Etty flew faster and higher. The air grew thin, and Ray began to slip. He couldn't hold on. With a gasp, Ray tumbled down into the storm.

DYK

When the ravens bother the eagles they simply fly higher and higher until they reach so high where the air gets thinner and the ravens give up as they cannot breathe.

Above the storm, the sky was calm and bright. Etty burst through the clouds and into the sunlight, where Ella, Ethan and Esty were waiting.

"You did it!" Esty cheered, circling with joy.

Ethan smiled wide. "I'm proud of you, Etty. You trusted your heart and flew with courage."

Etty flew beside them, his wings tired but strong. "I was scared... but I knew you were right, Dad. I just had to believe."

Ethan nodded. "Sometimes, others may speak with fear. But you must always remember the truth, your purpose—even when it's difficult."

Etty looked down at the storm below, then up at the peaceful sky around him.

He felt brave. He felt free.

And he knew—he was born to soar!

"...but those who hope in the Lord will renew their strength. They will soar on wings like eagles; they will run and not grow weary; they will walk and not be faint." - Isaiah 40:31

"I CARRY YOU ON EAGLES' WINGS AND BRING YOU TO MYSELF."

– FATHER GOD

Exodus 19:4